NATURE IN FOCUS

LIFE IN A BACKYARD

By Jen Green

Gareth Stevens Publishing

Please visit our Web site www.garethstevens.com. For a free color catalog of all our high-quality books, call toll free 1-800-542-2595 or fax 1-877-542-2596.

Library of Congress Cataloging-in-Publication Data
Green, Jen.
    Life in a backyard / Jen Green.
      p. cm. -- (Nature in focus)
    Includes index.
    ISBN 978-1-4339-3414-8 (library binding) -- ISBN 978-1-4339-3415-5 (pbk.)
    ISBN 978-1-4339-3416-2 (6-pack)
    1. Suburban animals--Juvenile literature. I. Title.
QH541.5.C6G74 2010
591.75'6--dc22
                                                      2009038715

Published in 2010 by
Gareth Stevens Publishing
111 East 14th Street, Suite 349
New York, NY 10003

© 2010 The Brown Reference Group Ltd.

For Gareth Stevens Publishing:
Art Direction: Haley Harasymiw
Editorial Direction: Kerri O'Donnell

For The Brown Reference Group Ltd:
Editorial Director: Lindsey Lowe
Managing Editor: Tim Harris
Editor: Jolyon Goddard
Children's Publisher: Anne O'Daly
Design Manager: David Poole
Designer: Lorna Phillips
Picture Manager: Sophie Mortimer
Picture Researcher: Clare Newman
Production Director: Alastair Gourlay

Picture Credits:
Front Cover: istockphoto; Shutterstock: Nikolay Okhitin (background)
FLPA: ImageBroker: 30; Piotr Naskrecki/Minden Pictures; 11; Getty Images: Comstock: 27b; istockphoto: 26-27; Jupiter Images: Photos.com: 28, 29b; Stockxpert: 20b; Shutterstock: Deborah Aronds: 23; Jorge Pedro Baradas de Casals: 10; Beata Becla:31; Mircea Bezergheanu: 21t; Ivan Bondarenko: 16; P Borowka:12t, Steve Bower: 4; Aron Brand: 9; Ferenc Cegledi: 22; Francesco Dazzi: 24; Elena Elisseeva: 3, 5; Arto Hakola: 18; idesign: 20t; Cathy Keifer: 13b; Mastering Microstock: 17; Kay Sim Seng: 8; Audrey Snider-Bell: 29t; Konstantin Sutyagin: 13t; Mary Terriberry: 14; Ron Waldrop: 19
All Artworks Brown Reference Group:

All rights reserved. No part of this book may be reproduced in any form without permission in writing from the publisher, except by a reviewer.

Manufactured in the United States of America
1 2 3 4 5 6 7 8 9   12 11 10

CPSIA compliance information: Batch #BRW0102GS: For further information contact Gareth Stevens, New York, New York at 1-800-542-2595.

Contents

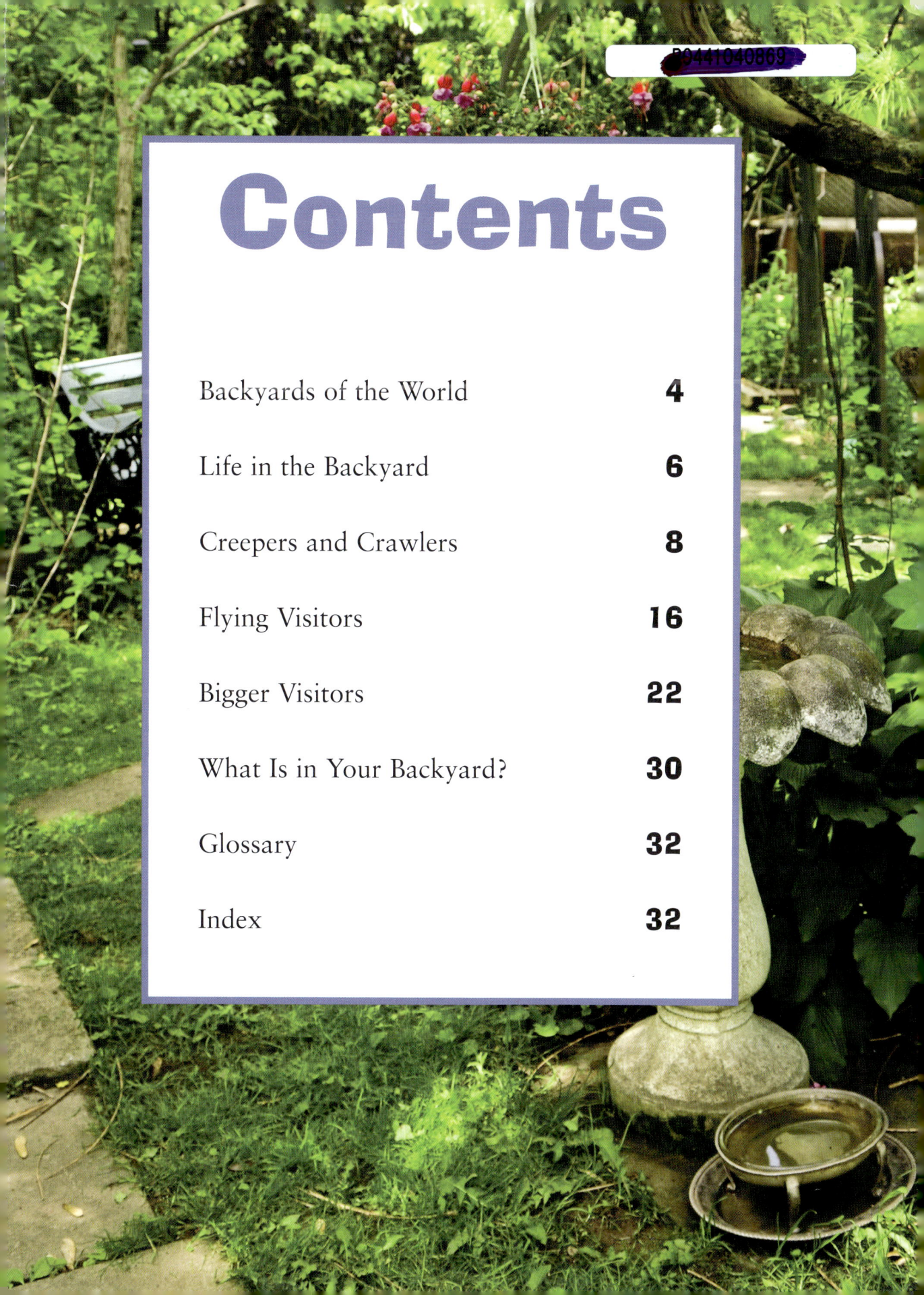

Backyards of the World	4
Life in the Backyard	6
Creepers and Crawlers	8
Flying Visitors	16
Bigger Visitors	22
What Is in Your Backyard?	30
Glossary	32
Index	32

Backyards of the World

Backyards around the world are home to many different kinds of animals, including mammals, birds, insects, reptiles, and amphibians. Some backyard animals are big, but most are small. This book will introduce you to some of the species, or types of animals, that live in or visit backyards in North America.

Coyotes are wild doglike animals that sometimes look for food in backyards.

Not all of the animals in your backyard are wild. Pet cats, for example, hunt in backyards for small birds and mammals.

Some types of animals prefer big, overgrown yards to live in. Others like tiny areas in crowded cities.

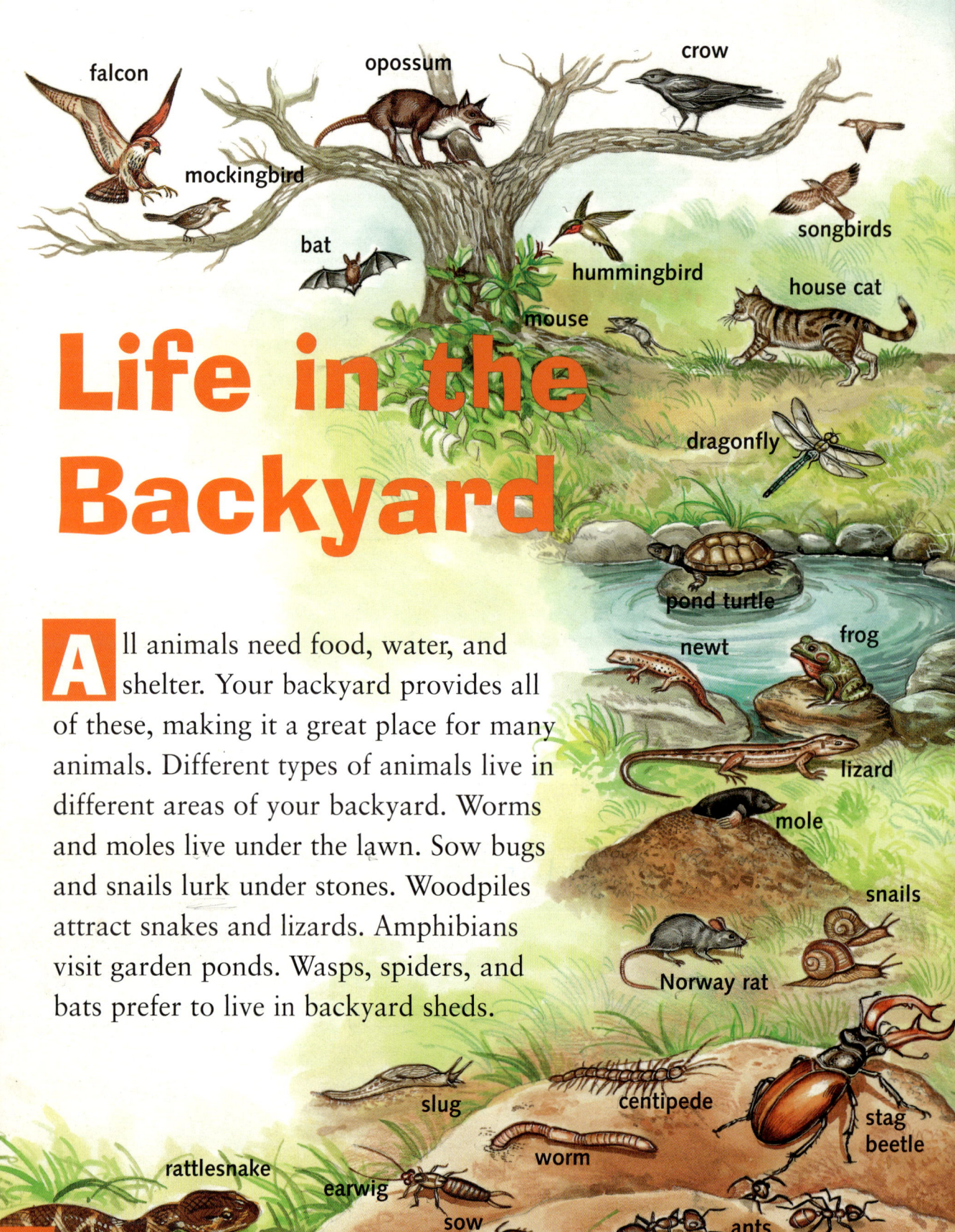

Life in the Backyard

All animals need food, water, and shelter. Your backyard provides all of these, making it a great place for many animals. Different types of animals live in different areas of your backyard. Worms and moles live under the lawn. Sow bugs and snails lurk under stones. Woodpiles attract snakes and lizards. Amphibians visit garden ponds. Wasps, spiders, and bats prefer to live in backyard sheds.

Creepers and Crawlers

The creepers and crawlers in your backyard include many insects, such as ants, beetles, and butterflies. Insects eat all kinds of foods, including plants and other insects. Some are pests, but others help gardeners. Some beetle grubs dig into logs and tree trunks to eat wood. Others eat dung or the remains of dead animals.

Dragonflies are often seen hovering near backyard ponds in summer.

The Beauties and the Pests

Beetles are the largest group of insects. They include ladybugs, weevils, and stag beetles. In spring, male stag beetles wrestle with each other for the chance to mate with a female.

Dragonflies often visit backyards with ponds. These fierce **predators** hunt other insects in midair. Butterflies have colorful wing markings. They feed on flower nectar, which they suck using long, strawlike mouthparts. Some insects are pests. Aphids damage plants by feeding on their sap.

Male stag beetles use their antlerlike mouthparts to fight each other.

Aphids release a sweet liquid called honeydew after sucking sap from plants.

Insect Colonies

All ants and some bees and wasps live in groups called colonies. In summer, you may discover an ants' nest in the backyard. The nest contains at least one large female ant, called the queen, who spends her time laying eggs. All the other ants are her children. They are mostly female workers, who care for the young ants and the queen. They also clean, guard the nest, and search for food outside. A beehive is similar to an ant colony. It has a queen bee, a few males called drones, and thousands of female workers.

Ants love sweet foods. They "milk" aphids for honeydew and sometimes collect the aphids to keep near their nest.

These worker ants are carrying a larva (a young developing ant) to a place of greater safety in their nest.

Life in a Backyard

Busy Bees

Worker bees collect nectar from flowers and bring it back to the nest to make honey. They also collect pollen to eat. As the bees fly from plant to plant, they carry pollen from one flower to another, helping the plants make their seeds.

Only older honeybees leave the hive to collect nectar and pollen.

CYCLE OF LIFE

Bees, beetles, ants, and butterflies have four-stage life cycles. From eggs, they hatch into caterpillars or legless grubs. These larvae feed and grow and become **pupae**, after which they emerge as adults. The change from larva to adult is called metamorphosis. Butterfly pupae are also called chrysalises. The diagram at right shows the life cycle of the monarch butterfly.

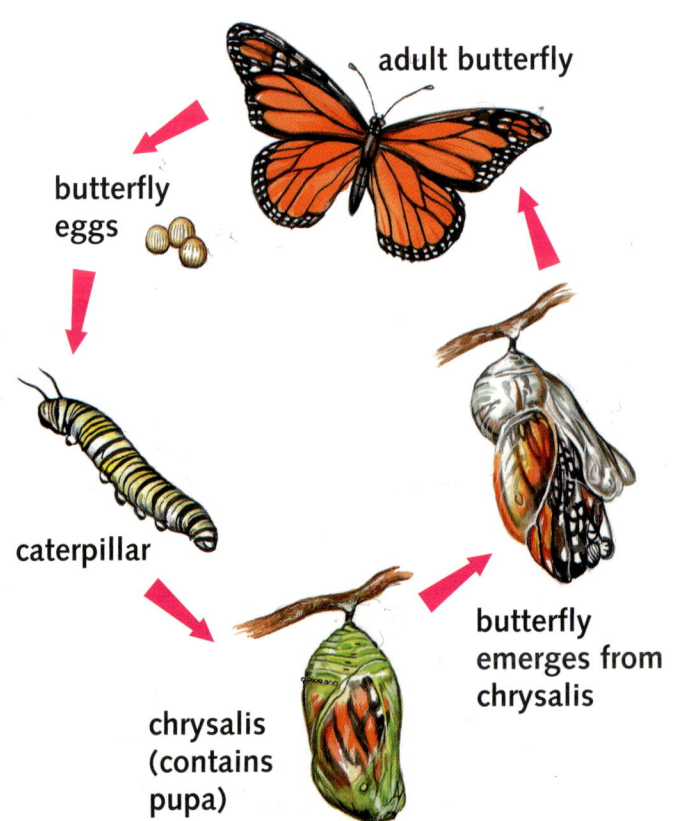

Creepers and Crawlers

Ladybugs help gardeners by feeding on pesky sap-sucking aphids.

Summer Sights
You will see more insects in your backyard in summer than in winter. Queen wasps, ladybugs, and butterflies live in sheds and woodpiles in winter, but the cold kills most adult insects. Although many of the adults do not make it, their eggs and pupae survive in the soil and hatch the next spring.

The Backyard at Night
Many backyard animals cannot be seen during the day. Snails, sow bugs, centipedes, and many others are mostly **nocturnal**, or active at night. Moths are night flyers. They are attracted to light and flutter around windows. Fireflies (right) flash their little lights. Flashing is the way that fireflies speak to each other and attract mates.

Hideaways and Hunters

Sow bugs and centipedes hide under stones during the day and look for food at night. Centipedes are predators. They hunt small insects. Sow bugs feed on rotting plants.

Spiders belong to the group of animals called arachnids. Spiders hunt insects and other spiders for food. Many spiders catch their prey by weaving webs of sticky thread. Most spiders paralyze their prey by injecting poison, or **venom**, with their fangs.

Banded garden spiders live in yards across most of North America. They catch flying insects in their sticky webs, which they spin across bushes.

Although they look a little like beetles, sow bugs are not insects. They are related to water-living crabs, shrimp, and lobsters.

Creepers and Crawlers

SLUGS, SNAILS, AND WORMS

Slugs and snails are invertebrates, or animals without a spine, and they have soft, slimy bodies. Snails have a hard shell for protection, but slugs have only a small shell inside their body or no shell at all. They move along on their flat bellies, leaving a slimy trail. At night, slugs and snails eat plants, especially new leaves. Most gardeners see slugs and snails as pests.

Earthworms (below) are long, thin, legless animals that live in the soil. A large backyard might contain thousands of worms! Worms tunnel through the earth by swallowing soil and digesting the plant and animal matter it contains. The waste soil passes through the worm's body and is pushed up to the ground's surface, leaving a wormcast on the lawn. Unlike most slugs and snails, worms are very good for the backyard.

Flying Visitors

Birds are among the most colorful animals to visit your backyard. At dusk, you can also see bats, as they hunt moths and other insects flying in the darkening sky. Most of the birds that come to your backyard are songbirds. This large group includes cardinals, wrens, crows, starlings, chickadees, thrushes, and finches.

Starlings flock together. They feed on seeds, worms, insects, and snails.

Different songbirds have different songs, so birds of the same type can recognize each other.

Blue jays, such as this chick, are among the noisiest birds to visit backyards.

Five U.S. states have northern mockingbirds as their state bird.

Beautiful Birdsong

Songbirds are also known as perching birds. Their feet have three toes facing forward and one facing backward. This arrangement helps the birds grip tightly around branches, so they do not fall off when resting at night.

The beautiful sounds of songbirds can be heard in most backyards, even in big cities. Their chorus is loud in the evening and even louder at dawn, when the birds wake up. Mockingbirds are songbirds that mimic the calls of other birds and can be heard in backyards across North America.

Male mockingbirds sing all day and sometimes at night.

Flying Visitors

Color in the Backyard

Cardinals, bluebirds, and robins are among the most colorful songbirds that visit your backyard. Like many bird species, the females are less colorful than the males. For example, female eastern bluebirds are very dull in color, but males have a bright blue back and a red chest. The males are bright to attract and impress the females. The females need dull colors to hide when sitting in their nests.

Songbirds sing to let other birds know they are in the area.

This northern cardinal is easy to identify as a male because it is bright red. The female cardinal has brown feathers.

Life in a Backyard

Tiny Birds

Hummingbirds are tiny, dainty birds that brighten backyards during spring and summer. They are named for the humming sounds their wings make as they flutter up and down at great speed. Their flapping wings help the birds hover, or stay still in the air. Hummingbirds build tiny, cup-shaped nests in which they lay their tiny eggs.

A hummingbird's long beak helps it reach the sweet nectar at the heart of a flower.

Nesting Times

Throughout the seasons, birds follow a breeding cycle. As the weather warms in spring, the birds sing loudly to find mates and set up breeding areas. Then they pair up, build their nests, and lay their eggs. When the eggs hatch, parent birds bring food to the nestlings, or baby birds. In summer, you can see young birds practicing their flying skills.

Flying Visitors

Like crows, magpies often raid other birds' nests and steal their eggs.

Other Bird Visitors

Blue jays, magpies, and crows are all related. These intelligent birds feed on a wide range of foods, including insects, reptiles, frogs, and small mammals. Some bird species in your backyard live there all year. Others, such as swallows, may drop in to your yard as they fly north or south on long migrations.

FLYING MAMMALS

Bats are flying mammals that often visit backyards to hunt. They are nocturnal and **roost** in sheds, attics, or hollow trees during the daylight hours. Some bats cannot see well, but all bats have excellent hearing. They track their prey using echolocation. As the bat flies through the air, it produces high-pitched clicking sounds. The sound waves from these clicks spread out and bounce off objects such as flying insects. The bat listens for the returning echoes, targets its prey, and swoops in for the kill.

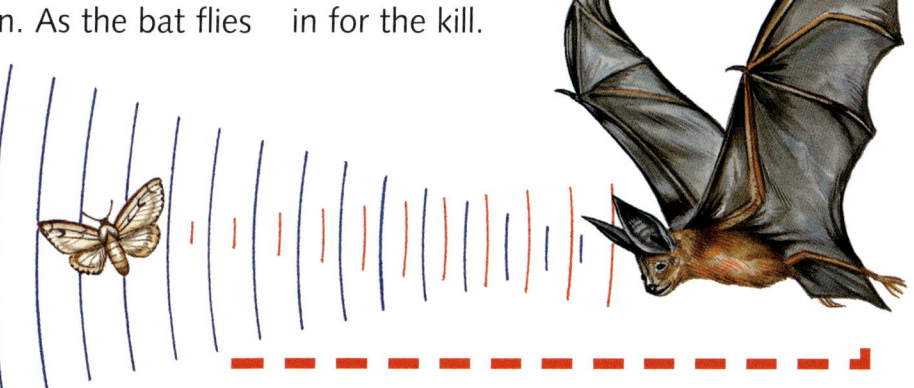

This bat uses echolocation to catch a moth in midair.

21

Bigger Visitors

Bigger backyard visitors include mammals, reptiles, and amphibians. Mammals have fur and feed their young on milk. They include bats, rodents such as mice and squirrels, raccoons, and skunks. Reptiles have scaly skins and include snakes, lizards, and turtles. Amphibians have moist skins and include frogs and salamanders.

With dark face markings like masks, raccoons look like bandits.

Rats live close to areas where there is plenty of garbage and other scraps to feed on.

At about seven weeks old, a young squirrel leaves its nest and explores its surroundings for the first time.

Nibblers and Gnawers

All rodents have strong teeth called incisors. They are used for biting and gnawing. Mice and squirrels are mainly plant eaters, gnawing on nuts, seeds, and buds. Rats eat both plant and animal matter. Rodents live in different places in the backyard. Rats and mice find shelter in sheds. Gophers are burrowing rodents that live underground. Squirrels live in the trees. Unlike most of the other mammals that visit, squirrels are **diurnal**, or active during the day.

Like all rodents, chipmunks use their constantly growing teeth to gnaw their food.

During the 1300s, rat fleas spread a deadly plague, called the Black Death, in Europe.

Bigger Visitors

Unpopular Guests

Moles are among the least popular animals that move into backyards. Many gardeners do not like the mole's tunneling activities because they leave mounds called molehills on the lawn. This small burrowing animal has strong front paws and long claws, which dig and shovel the earth at the same time. You may also see raccoons, foxes, and opossums in you backyard, even if you live in a city. At night, these visitors rummage through the garbage for food.

Wolves were frequent—although unwelcome—visitors to New York City 200 years ago! Local officials received a payment for every wolf that residents shot.

Moles are expert tunnelers. They have poor eyesight and rely on their sensitive noses to find tasty worms.

Collared lizards are brightly colored reptiles. They feed on other lizards and insects. This one is basking on a rock.

Lizard Life

Snakes, lizards, turtles, and alligators are all types of reptiles. Most of these scaly-skinned animals breed by laying eggs. Lizards are generally small reptiles, most common in warm areas, such as the southern United States and Mexico. Lizards sun themselves on rocks, on backyard walls, or dart across the yard chasing insects. Some male lizards expand a brightly colored patch of skin under their head, called a dewlap. They often do little push-ups at the same time. These behaviors warn other lizards to stay away from the performer's **territory** or their mates.

Virginia opossums are frequent visitors to backyards. Opossums are marsupials and are therefore relatives of the kangaroos in Australia.

Bigger Visitors

Slithering Snakes

Lizards are usually welcome visitors in our backyards, but snakes are mostly discouraged. Many people are frightened of snakes because some are venomous—they can give a poisonous bite. However, most snakes do not harm humans. Some people like snakes, because they eat pests such as mice and rats. Some species, such as the scarlet king snake, even feed on venomous snakes!

Forest Mammals

If you live near woods, your yard might be visited by deer and skunks. Deer are large mammals, but their brown or spotted coats provide such good **camouflage** that these shy animals are seldom seen. Skunks are more obvious, with their black and white stripes. Be careful around skunks—they squirt a foul-smelling spray at intruders!

Life in a Backyard

Amphibians

Frogs, toads, salamanders, and newts are amphibians. These are animals with moist skins that live in water and on land. Almost all amphibians live in ponds, lakes, streams, or rivers when young. Some amphibians spend all their adult life in water, too. But most adults leave the water for a life on land, returning to water only during the breeding season. Amphibians are predators that use their long, sticky tongues to capture passing insects and worms.

Many frogs have pouches in their throats that they fill with air to make their calls even louder during the mating season.

Tiger salamanders are the largest salamanders that live on land. They hunt insects and worms, and rest in moist burrows.

Croaky Critters

In spring, you can hear the loud, croaking sounds frogs and some toads make to attract mates. The females lay their gel-covered eggs in ponds and streams. The eggs hatch into plump, legless tadpoles, which swim by wriggling their long tail. After about eight weeks, the tadpole sprouts back legs, then front legs. The tadpole's tail shrinks as it slowly changes into an adult frog or toad.

If you have a pond in your backyard, it might be visited by a toad.

DANGEROUS SNAKES

Some regions in North America are home to venomous snakes, including cottonmouths, coral snakes, and rattlesnakes (left). Rattlesnakes are named for the "rattle" of loose scales on their tail, which they shake to frighten intruders away. Rattlesnakes are also known as pit vipers because of the heat-sensitive pits on their heads. The snakes use their heat sensors to track warm-blooded prey, such as mice, even in the dark, late at night.

What Is in Your Backyard?

There are several ways that you can attract wildlife to your backyard. To welcome birds, put food on a hanging bird table. The birds can feed safely there, away from cats and other backyard predators. Birds will eat all kinds of kitchen scraps, including bread, cheese, and bacon rind. Do not leave these treats out

A good way to feed birds is to place freshly cut fruit on a tree in your backyard.

in early summer, when they can choke nestlings. If hummingbirds are summer visitors, you can attract them to your yard by using a feeder (you can buy one from a pet store). Grow sweet-smelling plants to attract moths and butterflies to your backyard. Moths will visit if you plant honeysuckle, which smells strongly at night. Butterflies flock around verbena and wallflowers. You can also ask your parents to plant a buddleia, or butterfly bush.

TOP TIPS FOR ANIMAL WATCHERS

1 Binoculars can help you see distant animals. A magnifying glass will help you see small animals close up.

2 Most of the animals in your yard are easily scared off. Keep as still and quiet as possible. Get behind a bush to watch mammals and birds.

3 You will need a shaded flashlight to study nocturnal animals. If you stick a piece of red cellophane over the glass of your flashlight, the light won't scare the animals away.

If you keep still and quiet, you can get up close to wild animals.

Life in a Backyard

Glossary

camouflage Colors and patterns that help an animal blend in with its surroundings.
diurnal This term describes animals that sleep at night and are active during the day.
migrate To make a seasonal journey to escape cold weather, find food, or reach a safe place to breed.
nocturnal This term describes animals that sleep during the day and are active at night.

predators Animals that hunt other animals for food.
pupae The life stage between insect larvae and adults, when insects rebuild their body.
roost When flying animals such as birds and bats rest.
territory A breeding or feeding area that an animal defends against other animals.
venom A poison some animals inject when they bite.

Index

ant 6, 8, 11, 12
aphid 7, 10, 11, 13
bat 6, 16, 21, 22
bee 7, 11, 12
blue jay 17, 21
bluebird 19
butterfly 7, 8, 9, 10, 12, 13, 31
cardinal 16, 19
centipede 6, 13, 14
chipmunk 7, 24
coyote 4
crow 6, 16, 21
deer 7, 27
dragonfly 6, 8, 10

firefly 13
frog 6, 22, 28, 29
garden spider 7, 14
gopher 24
hummingbird 6, 20, 31
ladybug 7, 10, 13
lizard 6, 22, 26, 27
magpie 21
mockingbird 6, 18
mole 6, 25
opossum 6, 25, 26
raccoon 7, 22, 25
rat 6, 7, 23, 24, 27
salamander 22, 28
skunk 7, 22, 27

slug 6, 15
snail 6, 13, 15, 16
snake 6, 22, 26, 27, 29
songbird 6, 16, 17, 18, 19
sow bug 6, 13, 14
squirrel 7, 22, 23, 24
stag beetle 6, 10
starling 16
toad 28, 29
turtle 6, 22, 26
wasp 11, 13
wolf 25
worm 6, 15, 16, 25, 28

32